GET WELL

Written By:
Herbert I. Kavet

Illustrated By:
Martin Riskin

Ivory Tower Publishing Co., Inc.
111 Bauer Drive, Oakland, NJ 07436

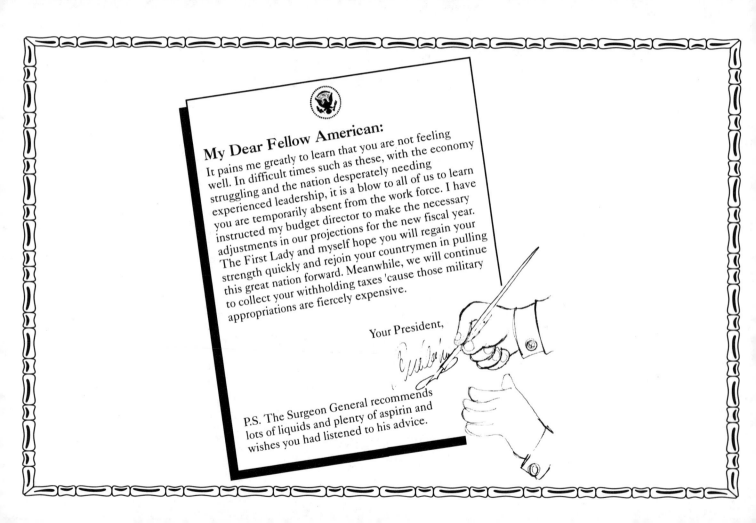

My Dear Fellow American:

It pains me greatly to learn that you are not feeling well. In difficult times such as these, with the economy struggling and the nation desperately needing experienced leadership, it is a blow to all of us to learn you are temporarily absent from the work force. I have instructed my budget director to make the necessary adjustments in our projections for the new fiscal year. The First Lady and myself hope you will regain your strength quickly and rejoin your countrymen in pulling this great nation forward. Meanwhile, we will continue to collect your withholding taxes 'cause those military appropriations are fiercely expensive.

Your President,

P.S. The Surgeon General recommends lots of liquids and plenty of aspirin and wishes you had listened to his advice.

HOW TO TELL IF YOU ARE REALLY SICK

How often has this happened to you? You wake up with your eyelids stuck together and sandy, your throat is scratchy, you feel vague, headachy feelings and you didn't even party the night before. You lie in bed trying to justify staying in bed. How can you determine if these symptoms represent an illness serious enough to stay home?

HOW TO TELL IF YOU ARE REALLY SICK

How to tell if you are really sick. This is easy. Ask yourself the following medically approved analytical questions.

1. Is the boss out of town?

2. Is it a great beach day?

3. Is an unfinished paper or major project due?

4. Is the weather inclement or very cold?

5. Is there fresh new powder for skiing?

6. Is there a nearby bed partner promising to make your head swim?

7. Is it Spring? Summer? Fall?

If any of your answers are yes, you are surely sick, and it would be a tremendous disservice to your friends and coworkers to expose them to your germs. Better stay home.

HOW TO TELL IF YOU ARE REALLY SICK

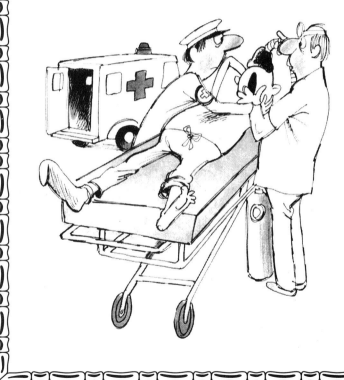

Suppose, however:

1. It's a weekend.

2. You have tickets to a great game or show.

3. It's pay day.

4. You have a super date for lunch.

5. An in-law is staying with you. AND you still feel droopy and headachy. This is considerably more serious. It appears that you are really, really sick, and you should get some competent medical attention at once.

What The Doctor Says:

"Wellllll, what have we here...?"

What The Doctor Really Means:

Since he hasn't the foggiest notion of what it is, the doctor is hoping you will give him a clue.

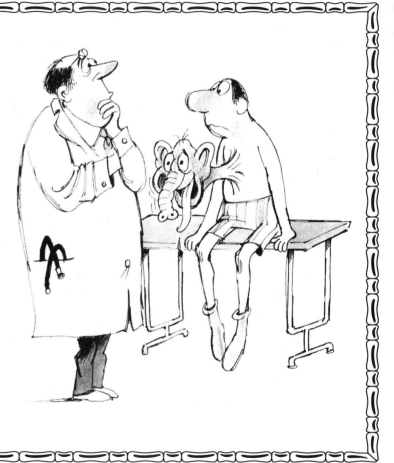

RECOGNIZING DOCTORS

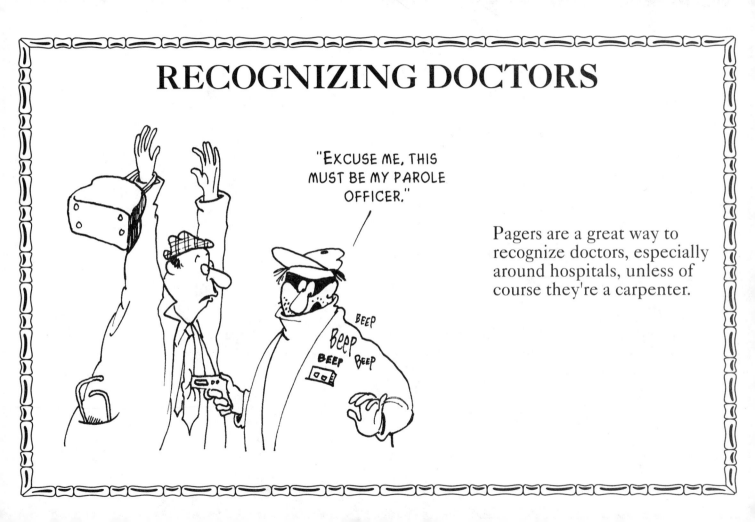

"EXCUSE ME, THIS MUST BE MY PAROLE OFFICER."

Pagers are a great way to recognize doctors, especially around hospitals, unless of course they're a carpenter.

What The Doctor Says:

"This should be taken care of right away."

What The Doctor Really Means:

"I'd planned a trip to Hawaii next month but this is so easy and profitable that I want to fix it before it cures itself."

THE NURSE

You're feeling lousy. The nurse is feeling great. This is obvious to you both. No matter. She has to say it. "And how are we feeling today?" The lady has employed a totally presumptuous and inappropriate editorial "we," permitting you to reply, in all good conscience "I feel like hell and I don't really give a damn how you feel." As with the little old lady who asked the four-year-old, "And how old are we?", and received the thoughtful reply, "A hundred and four?"

THE ORDERLY

If the orderly says nothing the whole time he is in the room while smiling continuously like a simpleton, the chances are that he does not speak English. He may have just gotten off the boat. He is smiling because he is in America. And who can blame him?

THE MORNING VISITOR

There is a morning visitor that you might watch for, too, who will be a little old lady in a hospital gown, using a walker and with toast crumbs on her upper lip, who will come rather wildly bumping her way into your room to announce gravely, "The Lord giveth, and the Lord taketh away." Do not be alarmed. She is talking to herself. She is referring to her marbles.

What The Doctor Says:

"We'll see."

What The Doctor Really Means:

"First I have to check my malpractice insurance."

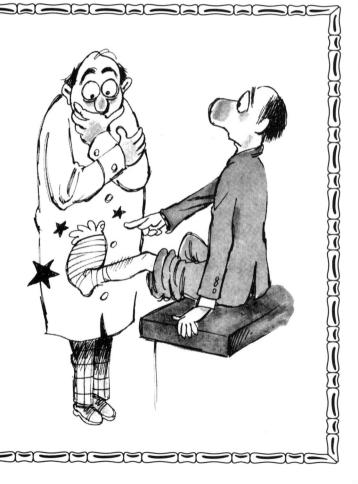

GERMS & CRITTERS
THAT MAKE YOU SICK

Tinglefuds

Cause tremendous gas
pressure in your bowels
whenever attractive members
of the opposite sex are about.

Schmendrik Snout

When angered by excessive
nose picking, these vindictive
little critters close and clog
nasal passages and make it
almost impossible to breathe.

GERMS & CRITTERS
THAT MAKE YOU SICK

Sogret

Never let two Sogrets get together. They will fight and bicker until they give you a migraine you will never forget.

The Chocorun

Bitterness, caused by lack of hot fudge brownies and chocolate eclairs by people on diets, stimulate this intestinal devil. He will keep you running between your bed and the toilet until you've lost enough weight to feel comfortable feeding him his favorites again.

GERMS & CRITTERS
THAT MAKE YOU SICK

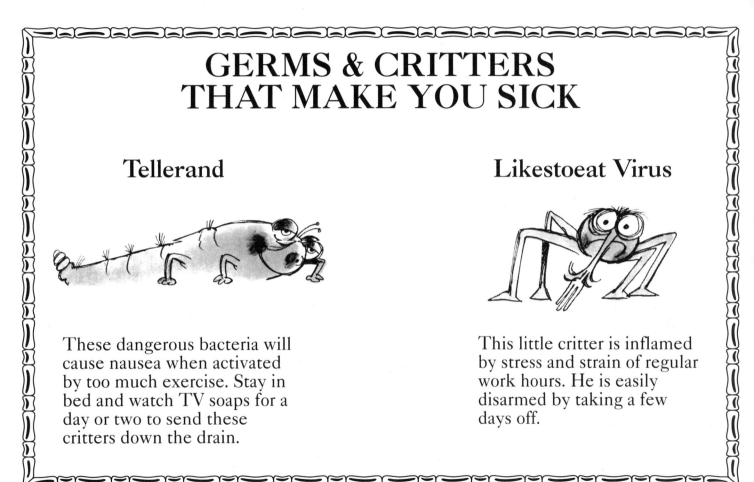

Tellerand

These dangerous bacteria will cause nausea when activated by too much exercise. Stay in bed and watch TV soaps for a day or two to send these critters down the drain.

Likestoeat Virus

This little critter is inflamed by stress and strain of regular work hours. He is easily disarmed by taking a few days off.

What The Doctor Says:

"Let me check your medical history."

What The Doctor Really Means:

"I want to see if you've paid your last bill before spending any more time with you.

BIOPSIES

For a biopsy, they usually snip off a tiny piece of tissue to test. Try to stay alert when they are doing this.

What The Doctor Says:

"Why don't you make an appointment later in the week."

What The Doctor Really Means:

"Wednesday I play golf."

What The Doctor Says:

"I really can't recommend seeing a chiropractor."

What The Doctor Really Means:

"I hate those guys mooching in on our fees."

CHIROPRACTORS

No matter what the ailment, the chiropractor always says the same thing to their patients. "There's an alignment problem in your back. Now this has been going on for a long time, but I can correct it. It's going to take some time, of course, to do the adjustments so you've got to commit to a program of visits." Then he tells you—in a conspiratorial tone—that one leg is 3/8" longer than the other. It's best to pick a chiropractor whose office is close by and with easy parking, because these visits go on for the rest of your life.

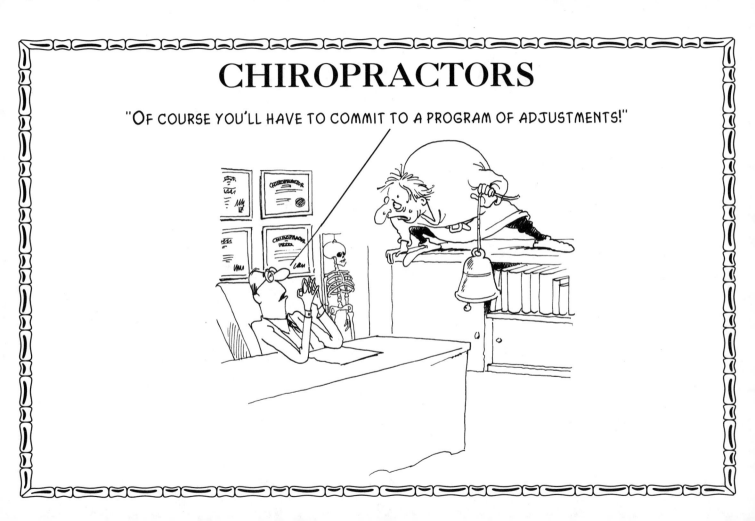

GAINING SYMPATHY

Gaining sympathy should be a primary objective of a sick person. Sympathy provides added care, quiet and consideration, more visitors, gifts and if handled correctly, can put sufficient guilt on your family and friends to carry over weeks and months after you are totally recovered. Certain types of illnesses, of course, gather more sympathy than others, for example:

Poor Sympathy Potential

Cold

Bad Back

Headaches

Upset Stomach

Stiff Neck

Sore Throat

GAINING SYMPATHY

Good Sympathy Potential

Pneumonia

Anything Wrapped in Plaster

Migraines

Intestinal Dyspepsia

Cervical Sprain

Strep Throat

Sometimes just changing a word or two of your sickness can do wonders for sympathy. Diarrhea, for example, sounds disgusting and inconsequential, but mention dysentery, and everyone knows you are a person who has traveled the world.

GAINING SYMPATHY

Once you have a colorful description of your illness, the next step in gaining sympathy is the judicious use of grimaces, winces and whimpers.

The "Flash-of-Pain" Grimace

A fleeting contraction of the facial muscles, held for the count of two and waved off as "just something I've got to learn to live with."

The Involuntary Wince

Whenever anyone touches you—anywhere. Be forgiving. "I'm sorry, but it hurts so much."

GAINING SYMPATHY

The Stoic Whimper

Close your eyes, avert your face and let your body be racked with silent sobs for a long moment, then whisper, "Oh, my God."

Holding on 'til Your Knuckles Get White

To the sheets, to a rolled-up magazine, to the arm of the visitor, saying, "Wait a second, okay, it'll pass."

Clenching Your Teeth

An effective response to, "How do you feel?", accompanied by the answer, "Oh, not so bad, I guess."

MAKING SURE YOU ARE REALLY SICK

To make sure you are really sick and not just looking for companionship, doctors like to have you pee in little bottles and give them blood samples.

"WELL, WE DON'T USUALLY ANESTHETIZE FOR BLOOD TESTS."

LAWYERS MUST BE ESPECIALLY WARY WHEN THEY ARE SICK.

"ATTORNEY FLENIBECK WOULD LIKE ONE MORE ASSURANCE THAT YOU WON'T USE THE RUSTY SCALPEL YOU THREATENED HIM WITH IN COURT LAST WEEK."

What The Doctor Says:

"Hmmmmmmmmmmmm."

What The Doctor Really Means:

Since he hasn't the faintest idea of what to do, he is trying to appear thoughtful while hoping the nurse will interrupt. (Proctologists also say this a lot.)

What The Doctor Says:

"We have some good news and some bad news."

What The Doctor Really Means:

The good news is he's going to buy that new BMW, and the bad news is that you're going to pay for it.

What The Doctor Says:

"Let's see how it develops."

What The Doctor Really Means:

"Maybe in a few days it will grow into something that can be cured."

WHEN YOU ARE TRYING TO SLEEP

You dog will get into a fight with another animal. This is true even if you don't have a dog. Though you live in an ecological wasteland and there hasn't been a chirping bird heard for a season, one will screech outside your window. Neighborhood kids will bounce tennis balls off the sides of your apartment even though you live on the 26th floor. If you live on a houseboat, anchored twelve miles out to sea, honking cars will still wake you. Don't ask me to explain it, these things just happen.

THE LONE VISITOR

In large hospitals, you may encounter
the lone visitor who comes and just sits
and looks at you. Never says a word.
Usually, a middle-aged woman with
long, stringy hair. You never saw her
before in your life. You figure she must
be some kind of a nut. You hope so,
anyhow.

THE VISITORS

Then there are those who choose to visit you en masse. Usually it's the gang where you work. None of them wished to come alone on account of they don't know what to say to sick people. So they come in a group and not a one of them knows what to say, so they all just stand there with a look on their faces as though they were about to dissect a frog. You can only hope they feel good about it later; but it will be quite awhile after they leave before you stop feeling like a frog.

THE VISITORS

Or there is a crowd that comes to see
you straight from the greatest party ever.
They are, every one of them, smashed
out of their minds. They come into your
room on a great tide of hilarity, reeking
of booze. Sure enough, you strike them
as really comical as hell, lying there in
bed, playing dead and all. Every one of
them will use the john before they
leave. You may wonder if that was all
they came for. You'll be lucky if none of
them throws up. Cheers!

MEDICAL ADVICE

Free and convenient
medical advice is usually
available at any large party.

What The Doctor Says:

"I'd like to have my associate look at you."

What The Doctor Really Means:

"He's going through a messy divorce and owes me a small fortune."

PILLS

Pills range from little, round, slippery, good tasting ones which are no problem to take, to giant, dry capsules filled with throat-choking, vile medicine which are more terrifying than rectal thermometers. The only problem with the little, round, slippery ones is that it is impossible to only roll one out of the bottle at a time. By the time you pick the extras off the floor and out of your wet palm and put them back in the little bottle, they are so contaminated as to be practically valueless.

The size and coating of a pill have nothing to do with its strength or effectiveness. The size is determined by available machine time at the pharmaceutical company. If the horse pill machine is available on the day your anti-inflammatory drug is being made, that is likely the size you'll get.

What The Doctor Says:

"Let me schedule you for some tests."

What The Doctor Really Means:

"I have a 40% interest in the lab."

Once you are feeling better, stories about your illness will thrill your friends for years.

MOM AS DOCTOR

When you are feeling sick, a Mom should be your first line of defense.

Moms:

1. Prescribe old folk remedies (like chicken soup) which usually work.

2. Make house calls.

3. Can be reached at any hour and don't use a beeper.

4. Continue to advise you and her other patients with constant follow-ups.

MOM AS DOCTOR

Moms, of course, do have a few weaknesses due to their lack of formal training.

1. She specializes in where the patient caught the cold rather than how to cure it.

2. She spends an inordinate amount of time with questions about nutrition and warm clothes.

3. Often cuts off discussion with "I told you so."

4. She thinks she knows everything but never does tests.

5. She keeps current by reading women's magazines and watching "20/20."

What The Doctor Says:

"How are we today?"

What The Doctor Really Means:

"I feel great. You, on the other hand, look like hell."

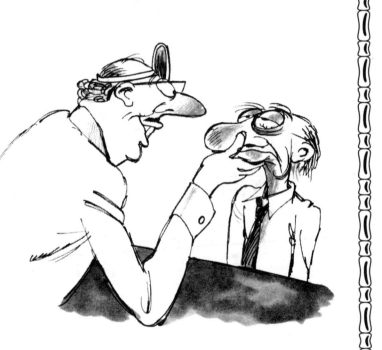

What The Doctor Says:

"I'd like to prescribe a new drug."

What The Doctor Really Means:

"I'm writing a paper and would like to use you for a guinea pig."

PATIENT'S GUIDE TO ANTACIDS

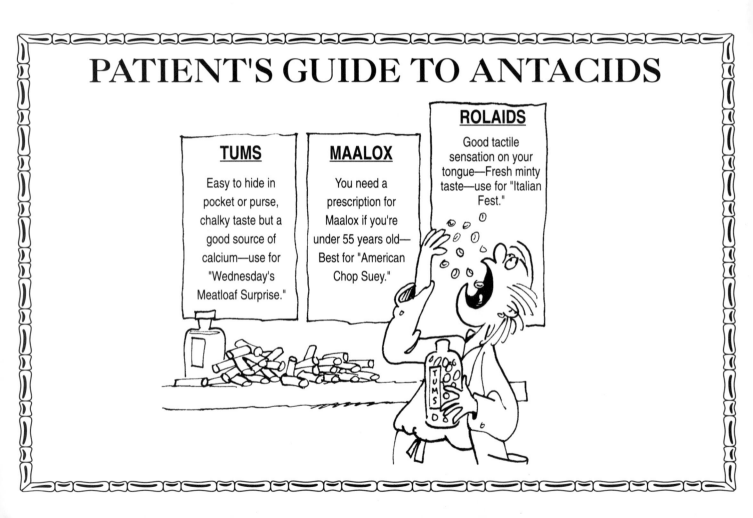

What The Doctor Says:

"If it doesn't clear up in a week, give me a call."

What The Doctor Really Means:

"I don't know what the hell it is. Maybe it will go away by itself."

What The Doctor Says:

"That's quite a nasty looking wound."

What The Doctor Really Means:

"I think I'm going to throw up."

NOCTURNAL SOUND I.D. CHART

If your illness requires a hospital stay, there is nothing more disconcerting than the strange noises you hear at night. This nocturnal sound chart will give you an idea of what these noises mean.

EH, EH, EH!

This is a 70-year-old woman with a 98.6° bottom sitting on a 34° bed pan.

EEEEEEEE-OO-O

Two and a half yards of adhesive bandage being removed from four inches of hairy skin.

NOCTURNAL SOUND I.D. CHART

AAAAAA-RG

A patient trying to swallow three aspirin that have already begun to dissolve in her mouth.

OO-OO-OO-OO

A burly nurse inserting a cold rectal thermometer without the use of a lubricant.

Yi Yi Yi Yi YAH!

A 92-year-old gall bladder case being fed beef broth through his nose.

ARE VITAMINS & MINERALS GOOD FOR YOU?

Medical and nutritional experts are absolutely positive about which vitamins and minerals are indispensable to your health and well-being, and they only change their minds every few days. If you buy your vitamins on the day IRON is still good for you and read that week's newspaper story about how it causes heart attacks, you're a goner. One man from Minnesota didn't get the word on MERCURY in swordfish and ended up as a thermometer in a gas station. This is a true story.

ARE VITAMINS & MINERALS GOOD FOR YOU?

Vitamin pills contain stuff like iron, manganese, chromium, iodine (if you can believe it), boron, tin and other things that are usually used to make cars, golf clubs and the like. It's no wonder people gain weight as they grow older. Do you suppose any of these minerals are really digestible? I would think all the minerals just accumulate and before you know it, you have iron bottoms, lead feet and hips made out of molybdenum.

WHAT ARE VITAMINS ANYWAY?

Vitamins are little letters that are invented by clever scientists working for pharmaceutical companies. They sell you these letters after they take them out of things like anchovy pizza and orange Tic Tacs, keeping the good parts for themselves. It's the free enterprise way and very important in a capitalistic society.

WHAT ARE VITAMINS ANYWAY?

Norman wondered if the vitamin K would really improve his sex life as much as the ad promised.

HOW TO EAT YOURSELF REGULAR

This hitherto unmentionable subject is printed here for the first time by the same clever fellow who brought you the Fart Books. We're talking about constipation here. "Regular" is only a polite term for the real problem which is CONSTIPATION. Constipation is caused by eating too much butterscotch, gum drops and Midwestern garlic bagels.

It can be reversed by the following methods:

Pry it loose with prune juice.

Finagle it out with figs.

Loosen it with laxatives.

Blast it out with bran.

Fix it yourself with fiber.

HOW TO EAT YOURSELF REGULAR

Herman finds that bran and natural fiber have an amazing effect on his regularity.

What The Doctor Says:

"This may smart a little."

What The Doctor
Really Means:

"Last week, two patients bit
through their tongues."

What The Doctor Says:

"Well, we're not feeling so well today, are we?"

What The Doctor Really Means:

"I can't remember your name, nor why you are here."

What The Doctor Says:

"This should fix you up."

What The Doctor Really Means:

"The drug salesman guaranteed that it kills all symptoms."

WHERE COLDS COME FROM

My mother was much more interested in
figuring out the exact place and moment
that you caught a cold than in curing it.
Whole family meetings were held with
aunts and uncles to determine just how
you caught it. "It was when his hair got
wet at Aunt Sophie's." "No, no, it was
when he didn't wear his sweater on that
windy day." Other aunts would argue for
hours about which parts of the body were
the most important to keep warm.

WHERE COLDS COME FROM

Nowadays, of course, science has explained that colds are carried by germs and viruses. You get these germs mostly from sitting on dirty toilet seats, so if you don't want to catch colds, you should always put down paper like your mother taught you.

What The Doctor Says:

"Everything seems to be normal."

What The Doctor Really Means:

"I guess I can't buy that new beach condominium after all."

PATIENT'S GUIDE TO LITTLE KNOWN GLANDS & ORGANS

SPINAX

"A Spinax can make you full of pain," said Isaac Lonken, a noted Tibetan healer. "Itzy" was right. Let's say a construction derrick falls on you. Then the Spinax takes over and fills you full of a lot of pain. Watch out for your Spinax.

BUFO VIRIDIS

"Buffy," as this organ is known in the anatomical trade, is a robust little sac of green corpuscles responsible for the greenish skin color during nausea.

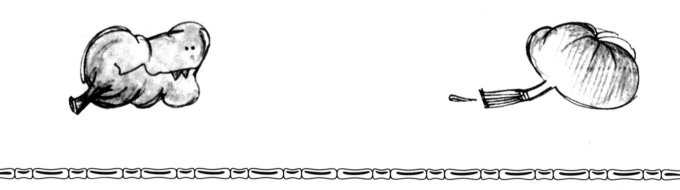

PATIENT'S GUIDE TO LITTLE KNOWN GLANDS & ORGANS

DACTELYNUM

The skinny little tube that when irritated, will encourage growth of hair in the mouth and throat. Never, never annoy the Dactelynum if you don't want a fuzzy tongue.

TUBMAN'S TEAT

A small duct located over the heart. Tubman's Teat is stimulated by boredom when driving a car and causes an uncontrollable urge to pick your nose.

VOLNIC BUTTON

This happy-go-lucky little gland or protuberance when pressed, will convulse into a tearful spasm of giggling. So never press your Volnic during periods that require serious attentiveness.

PATIENT'S GUIDE TO LITTLE KNOWN GLANDS & ORGANS

TRIGULA

A small, round muscular ball located in the upper digestive system which disperses tiny hemorrhoidal armies into the bowel canals to make constipation as painful as possible and to teach you a lesson.

DANDINUS ROKE

Also known as the Toke Roke, which releases spasms during pot smoking.

LATHYMUR

A proteal gland in the upper palate which secretes tartar deposits into teeth.

PATIENT'S GUIDE TO LITTLE KNOWN GLANDS & ORGANS

CORNUBALIS

A tiny but very cute little gland located in the foot which secretes material that ultimately degenerates into common foot corns and blisters.

RHOMB

This highly intelligent organ regulates flow of sperm during ejaculation. Be nice to your Rhomb, otherwise it will shut you off. Your Rhomb is very sensitive and it's feelings are hurt easily.

PATIENT'S GUIDE TO LITTLE KNOWN GLANDS & ORGANS

RUMPEAS

The gland that was discovered by Sidney Rumpeas, which secretes juices that make people go to the bathroom at the most inopportune times, mostly when 20 miles from the nearest john.

THYMBLE GUT

Twin glands of the intestinal tract which helps the body assimilate large amounts of Chinese food and makes you hungry one hour after eating it.

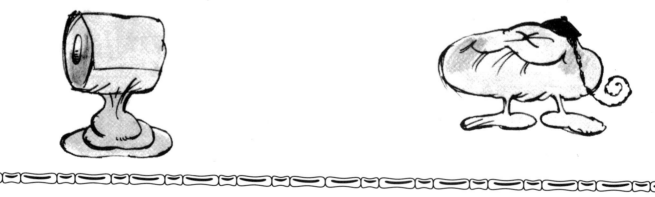

PATIENT'S GUIDE TO LITTLE KNOWN GLANDS & ORGANS

SHLEGORUS

A shy gland, which when activated, causes knees to shake uncontrollably during stressful situations.

GELP

This gland is chiefly responsible for the lint deposits that accumulate in belly buttons.

What The Doctor Says:

"I'd like to run some more tests."

What The Doctor Really Means:

"I can't figure out what's wrong. Maybe the kid in the lab can solve this one."

What The Doctor Says:

"Do you suppose all of that stress could be affecting your nerves?"

What The Doctor Really Means:

He thinks you are crazy and is hoping to find a psychiatrist who will split fees.

GOOD HEALTH AND PIMPLES

Good health is always associated with a good complexion. Here's a list of things that have a bad reputation about causing pimples.

1. Chocolate
2. Honey roasted peanuts
3. Salami sandwiches
4. Not washing your hair
5. Green Tic Tacs

None of these things can possibly cause pimples.

GOOD HEALTH AND PIMPLES

"DIANE, NO ONE IS GOING TO NOTICE ONE LITTLE PIMPLE."

The real causes of pimples are:

1. R-rated movies.

2. Doing "you know what" under the covers.

3. Nightmares about taking school exams.

4. Saving Victoria's Secret and Frederick's of Hollywood catalogs.

5. Fantasizing about sex during work.

ARE FARTS HEALTHY?

Definitely. Farts are a very natural body function whose main purpose is to keep you from exploding when you have a little gas. Naturally, when you are on a first date or having dinner at your boss's house, you cannot fart, and thousands of people are killed each year exploding at times like these. If people would just realize that farting is a perfectly natural and acceptable act, just like picking your nose when you're stuck in traffic, thousands of lives would be saved.

ARE FARTS HEALTHY?

IS SEX HEALTHY?

Sex may be fine for making babies but the effect on a person's health, and especially mental health, is usually devastating.

Five problems with sex are:

1. Fear of rejection.

2. Realization of inadequacies.

3. Acute embarrassment.

4. Uncomfortable positions.

5. Difficult to dispose of partner afterwards.

IS SEX HEALTHY?

There are some definite benefits, however:

1. Great stories to tell your friends.

2. A splendid opportunity to test that condom you've been carrying for a year.

3. A great way to learn some very descriptive new words.

4. You'll definitely learn some new spots that feel real good.

5. Unless you're a complete dork, it'll be much easier to get a date Saturday night.

What The Doctor Says:

"Why don't you slip out of your things."

What The Doctor Really Means:

"I don't enjoy this any more than you do, but I've got to warm my fingers up somehow."

What The Doctor Says:

"If those symptoms persist, call for an appointment."

What The Doctor Really Means:

"I've never heard of anything so disgusting. Thank God I'm off next week."

SATURDAY MORNING AT THE EMERGENCY ROOM

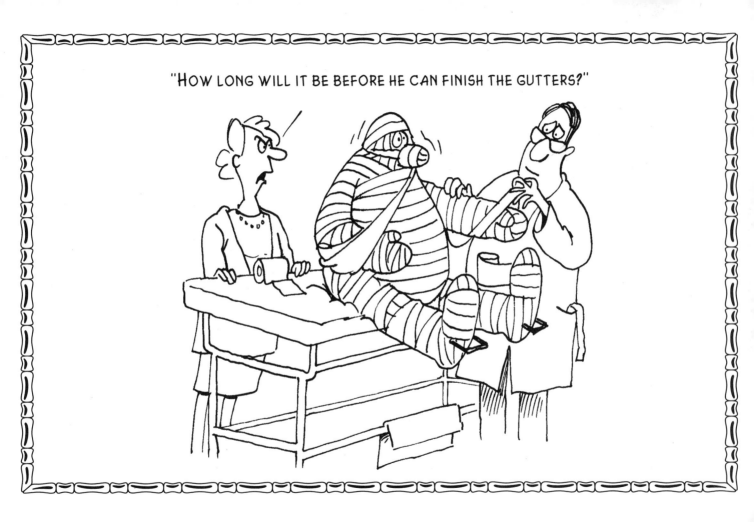

What The Doctor Says:

"There is a lot of that going around."

What The Doctor Really Means:

"My God, that's the third one this week. I'd better learn something about this."

10 GET WELL COMMANDMENTS

I. Thou shalt remember to properly fill out thy insurance forms.

II. Thou shalt bring lots of reading material to thy doctor's office, especially if thou visit a specialist.

III. Thou shalt not treat thyself with medications left over from last time.

IV. Thou shalt leave thy hospital before the food really maketh you sick.

V. Thou shalt buy presents for nurses because they are the ones that really know what's happening.

10 GET WELL COMMANDMENTS

VI. Thou shalt listen to thy mother because her advice is good.

VII. Thou shalt respect thy doctor, even those younger than thy kids.

VIII. Thou shalt always try to get thy prescription from the doctor's free samples.

IX. Thou shalt close thine eyes tight when giving blood samples.

X. Thou shalt not go to work if at all sick and spread germs amongst thy coworkers.